THE JPS B'NAI MITZVAH TORAH COMMENTARY

Naso' (Numbers 4:21–7:89)
Haftarah (Judges 13:2–25)

Rabbi Jeffrey K. Salkin

The Jewish Publication Society · Philadelphia
University of Nebraska Press · Lincoln

INTRODUCTION

News flash: the most important thing about becoming bar or bat mitzvah isn't the party. Nor is it the presents. Nor even being able to celebrate with your family and friends—as wonderful as those things are. Nor is it even standing before the congregation and reading the prayers of the liturgy—as important as that is.

No, the most important thing about becoming bar or bat mitzvah is sharing Torah with the congregation. And why is that? Because of all Jewish skills, that is the most important one.

Here is what is true about rites of passage: you can tell what a culture values by the tasks it asks its young people to perform on their way to maturity. In American culture, you become responsible for driving, responsible for voting, and yes, responsible for drinking responsibly.

In some cultures, the rite of passage toward maturity includes some kind of trial, or a test of strength. Sometimes, it is a kind of "outward bound" camping adventure. Among the Maasai tribe in Africa, it is traditional for a young person to hunt and kill a lion. In some Hispanic cultures, fifteen year-old girls celebrate the *quinceañera*, which marks their entrance into maturity.

What is Judaism's way of marking maturity? It combines both of these rites of passage: *responsibility* and *test*. You show that you are on your way to becoming a *responsible* Jewish adult through a public *test* of strength and knowledge—reading or chanting Torah, and then teaching it to the congregation.

This is the most important Jewish ritual mitzvah (commandment), and that is how you demonstrate that you are, truly, bar or bat mitzvah—old enough to be responsible for the mitzvot.

What Is Torah?

So, what exactly is the Torah? You probably know this already, but let's review.

The Torah (teaching) consists of "the five books of Moses," sometimes also called the *chumash* (from the Hebrew word *chameish,* which means "five"), or, sometimes, the Greek word Pentateuch (which means "the five teachings").

Here are the five books of the Torah, with their common names and their Hebrew names.

> **Genesis (The beginning), which in Hebrew is Bere'shit (from the first words—"When God began to create").** Bere'shit spans the years from Creation to Joseph's death in Egypt. Many of the Bible's best stories are in Genesis: the creation story itself; Adam and Eve in the Garden of Eden; Cain and Abel; Noah and the Flood; and the tales of the Patriarchs and Matriarchs, Abraham, Isaac, Jacob, Sarah, Rebekah, Rachel, and Leah. It also includes one of the greatest pieces of world literature, the story of Joseph, which is actually the oldest complete novel in history, comprising more than one-quarter of all Genesis.

> **Exodus (Getting out), which in Hebrew is Shemot (These are the names).** Exodus begins with the story of the Israelite slavery in Egypt. It then moves to the rise of Moses as a leader, and the Israelites' liberation from slavery. After the Israelites leave Egypt, they experience the miracle of the parting of the Sea of Reeds (or "Red Sea"); the giving of the Ten Commandments at Mount Sinai; the idolatry of the Golden Calf; and the design and construction of the Tabernacle and of the ark for the original tablets of the law, which our ancestors carried with them in the desert. Exodus also includes various ethical and civil laws, such as "You shall not wrong a stranger or oppress him, for you were strangers in the land of Egypt" (22:20).

> **Leviticus (about the Levites), or, in Hebrew, Va-yikra' (And God called).** It goes into great detail about the kinds of sacrifices that the ancient Israelites brought as offerings; the laws of ritual purity; the animals that were permitted and forbidden for eating (the beginnings of the tradition of kashrut, the Jewish dietary laws); the diagnosis of various skin diseases; the ethical laws of holiness; the ritual calendar of the Jewish year; and various agricultural laws concerning the treatment of the Land of Israel. Leviticus is basically the manual of ancient Judaism.

‣ **Numbers (because the book begins with the census of the Israelites), or, in Hebrew, Be-midbar (In the wilderness).** The book describes the forty years of wandering in the wilderness and the various rebellions against Moses. The constant theme: "Egypt wasn't so bad. Maybe we should go back." The greatest rebellion against Moses was the negative reports of the spies about the Land of Israel, which discouraged the Israelites from wanting to move forward into the land. For that reason, the "wilderness generation" must die off before a new generation can come into maturity and finish the journey.

‣ **Deuteronomy (The repetition of the laws of the Torah), or, in Hebrew, Devarim (The words).** The final book of the Torah is, essentially, Moses's farewell address to the Israelites as they prepare to enter the Land of Israel. Here we find various laws that had been previously taught, though sometimes with different wording. Much of Deuteronomy contains laws that will be important to the Israelites as they enter the Land of Israel—laws concerning the establishment of a monarchy and the ethics of warfare. Perhaps the most famous passage from Deuteronomy contains the *Shema,* the declaration of God's unity and uniqueness, and the *Ve-ahavta,* which follows it. Deuteronomy ends with the death of Moses on Mount Nebo as he looks across the Jordan Valley into the land that he will not enter.

Jews read the Torah in sequence—starting with Bere'shit right after Simchat Torah in the autumn, and then finishing Devarim on the following Simchat Torah. Each Torah portion is called a parashah (division; sometimes called a *sidrah,* a place in the order of the Torah reading). The stories go around in a full circle, reminding us that we can always gain more insights and more wisdom from the Torah. This means that if you don't "get" the meaning this year, don't worry—it will come around again.

And What Else? The Haftarah

We read or chant the Torah from the Torah scroll—the most sacred thing that a Jewish community has in its possession. The Torah is written without vowels, and the ability to read it and chant it is part of the challenge and the test.

But there is more to the synagogue reading. Every Torah reading has an accompanying haftarah reading. Haftarah means "conclusion," because there was once a time when the service actually ended with that reading. Some scholars believe that the reading of the haftarah originated at a time when non-Jewish authorities outlawed the reading of the Torah, and the Jews read the haftarah sections instead. In fact, in some synagogues, young people who become bar or bat mitzvah read very little Torah and instead read the entire haftarah portion.

The haftarah portion comes from the Nevi'im, the prophetic books, which are the second part of the Jewish Bible. It is either read or chanted from a Hebrew Bible, or maybe from a booklet or a photocopy.

The ancient sages chose the haftarah passages because their themes reminded them of the words or stories in the Torah text. Sometimes, they chose *haftarah* with special themes in honor of a festival or an upcoming festival.

Not all books in the prophetic section of the Hebrew Bible consist of prophecy. Several are historical. For example:

The book of Joshua tells the story of the conquest and settlement of Israel.

The book of Judges speaks of the period of early tribal rulers who would rise to power, usually for the purpose of uniting the tribes in war against their enemies. Some of these leaders are famous: Deborah, the great prophetess and military leader, and Samson, the biblical strong man.

The books of Samuel start with Samuel, the last judge, and then move to the creation of the Israelite monarchy under Saul and David (approximately 1000 BCE).

The books of Kings tell of the death of King David, the rise of King Solomon, and how the Israelite kingdom split into the Northern Kingdom of Israel and the Southern Kingdom of Judah (approximately 900 BCE).

And then there are the books of the prophets, those spokesmen for God whose words fired the Jewish conscience. Their names are immortal: Isaiah, Jeremiah, Ezekiel, Amos, Hosea, among others.

Someone once said: "There is no evidence of a biblical prophet ever being invited back a second time for dinner." Why? Because the prophets were tough. They had no patience for injustice, apathy, or hypocrisy. No one escaped their criticisms. Here's what they taught:

> God commands the Jews to behave decently toward one another. In fact, God cares more about basic ethics and decency than about ritual behavior.
> God chose the Jews *not* for special privileges, but for special duties to humanity.
> As bad as the Jews sometimes were, there was always the possibility that they would improve their behavior.
> As bad as things might be now, it will not always be that way. Someday, there will be universal justice and peace. Human history is moving forward toward an ultimate conclusion that some call the Messianic Age: a time of universal peace and prosperity for the Jewish people and for all the people of the world.

Your Mission—To Teach Torah to the Congregation

On the day when you become bar or bat mitzvah, you will be reading, or chanting, Torah—in Hebrew. You will be reading, or chanting, the haftarah—in Hebrew. That is the major skill that publicly marks the becoming of bar or bat mitzvah. But, perhaps even more important than that, you need to be able to teach something about the Torah portion, and perhaps the haftarah as well.

And that is where this book comes in. It will be a very valuable resource for you, and your family, in the b'nai mitzvah process.

Here is what you will find in it:

> A brief **summary** of every Torah portion. This is a basic overview of the portion; and, while it might not refer to everything in the Torah portion, it will explain its most important aspects.
> A list of the **major ideas** in the Torah portion. The purpose: to make the Torah portion real, in ways that we can relate to. Every Torah portion contains unique ideas, and when you put all

of those ideas together, you actually come up with a list of Judaism's most important ideas.

> Two *divrei Torah* ("words of Torah," or "sermonettes") for each portion. These *divrei Torah* explain significant aspects of the Torah portion in accessible, reader-friendly language. Each *devar Torah* contains references to **traditional** Jewish sources (those that were written before the modern era), as well as **modern** sources and quotes. We have searched, far and wide, to find sources that are unusual, interesting, and not just the "same old stuff" that many people already know about the Torah portion. Why did we include these minisermons in the volume? Not because we want you to simply copy those sermons and pass them off as your own (that would be cheating), though you are free to quote from them. We included them so that you can see what is possible—how you can try to make meaning for yourself out of the words of Torah.

> **Connections:** This is perhaps the most valuable part. It's a list of questions that you can ask yourself, or that others might help you think about—any of which can lead to the creation of your *devar Torah*.

Note: you don't have to like everything that's in a particular Torah portion. Some aren't that loveable. Some are hard to understand; some are about religious practices that people today might find confusing, and even offensive; some contain ideas that we might find totally outmoded.

But this doesn't have to get in the way. After all, most kids spend a lot of time thinking about stories that contain ideas that modern people would find totally bizarre. Any good medieval fantasy story falls into that category.

And we also believe that, if you spend just a little bit of time with those texts, you can begin to understand what the author was trying to say.

This volume goes one step further. Sometimes, the haftarah comes off as a second thought, and no one really thinks about it. We have tried to solve that problem by including a **summary** of each haftarah, and then a mini-sermon on the haftarah. This will help you learn how these sacred words are relevant to today's world, and even to your own life.

All Bible quotations come from the NJPS translation, which is found in the many different editions of the JPS TANAKH; in the Conservative movement's *Etz Hayim: Torah and Commentary;* in the Reform movement's *Torah: A Modern Commentary;* and in other Bible commentaries and study guides.

How Do I Write a *Devar Torah?*

It really is easier than it looks.

There are many ways of thinking about the *devar Torah*. It is, of course, a short sermon on the meaning of the Torah (and, perhaps, the haftarah) portion. It might even be helpful to think of the *devar Torah* as a "book report" on the portion itself.

The most important thing you can know about this sacred task is: *Learn* the words. *Love* the words. Teach people what it could mean to *live* the words.

Here's a basic outline for a *devar Torah:*

"My Torah portion is (name of portion) _____,
  from the book of _____ , chapter
  _____.
"In my Torah portion, we learn that_____
  (Summary of portion)
"For me, the most important lesson of this Torah portion is (what
  is the best thing in the portion? Take the portion as a whole;
  your *devar Torah* does not have to be only, or specifically, on the
  verses that you are reading).
"As I learned my Torah portion, I found myself wondering:
  ➤ *Raise a question that the Torah portion itself raises.*
  ➤ *"Pick a fight"* with the portion. Argue with it.
  ➤ *Answer a question* that is listed in the "Connections" section of
    each Torah portion.
  ➤ *Suggest a question to your rabbi* that you would want the rabbi
    to answer in his or her own *devar Torah* or sermon.

"I have lived the values of the Torah by _____
(here, you can talk about how the Torah portion relates to your
own life. If you have done a mitzvah project, you can talk about
that here).

How To Keep It from Being Boring
(and You from Being Bored)

Some people just don't like giving traditional speeches. From our perspective, that's really okay. Perhaps you can teach Torah in a different way—one that makes sense to you.

> Write an "open letter" to one of the characters in your Torah portion. "Dear Abraham: I hope that your trip to Canaan was not too hard . . ." "Dear Moses: Were you afraid when you got the Ten Commandments on Mount Sinai? I sure would have been . . ."
> Write a news story about what happens. Imagine yourself to be a television or news reporter. "Residents of neighboring cities were horrified yesterday as the wicked cities of Sodom and Gomorrah were burned to the ground. Some say that God was responsible . . ."
> Write an imaginary interview with a character in your Torah portion.
> Tell the story from the point of view of another character, or a minor character, in the story. For instance, tell the story of the Garden of Eden from the point of view of the serpent. Or the story of the Binding of Isaac from the point of view of the ram, which was substituted for Isaac as a sacrifice. Or perhaps the story of the sale of Joseph from the point of view of his coat, which was stripped off him and dipped in a goat's blood.
> Write a poem about your Torah portion.
> Write a song about your Torah portion.
> Write a play about your Torah portion, and have some friends act it out with you.
> Create a piece of artwork about your Torah portion.

The bottom line is: Make this a joyful experience. Yes—it could even be fun.

The Very Last Thing You Need to Know at This Point

The Torah scroll is written without vowels. Why? Don't *sofrim* (Torah scribes) know the vowels?

Of course they do.

So, why do they leave the vowels out?

One reason is that the Torah came into existence at a time when sages were still arguing about the proper vowels, and the proper pronunciation.

But here is another reason: The Torah text, as we have it today, and as it sits in the scroll, is actually *an unfinished work*. Think of it: the words are just sitting there. Because they have no vowels, it is as if they have no voice.

When we read the Torah publicly, we give voice to the ancient words. And when we find meaning in those ancient words, and we talk about those meanings, those words jump to life. They enter our lives. They make our world deeper and better.

Mazal tov to you, and your family. This is your journey toward Jewish maturity. Love it.

THE TORAH

❖ Naso': Numbers 4:21–7:89

Welcome to the longest parashah in the entire Torah! Moses finishes up the census in order to figure out who is available for various tasks. Once he finishes with that, he goes back to creating the rules that will guide the future life of the Israelites.

The Torah portion describes two ancient customs that no longer exist: the "trial by ordeal" of women who are suspected of adultery, and the role of the Nazirite, a person who decides to go several steps beyond the usual rules of holiness and live a more ascetic life, cut off from many human temptations.

By the time this Torah portion ends, it is time for the dedication of the Tabernacle, the Tent of Meeting (*mishkan*), with a list of every person who brings gifts to the dedication, and the gifts that they bring. Oddly enough, they all bring the same things.

Summary

- ▸ The task of taking the census continues. Moses breaks the Levite clan into further subgroupings, describing the tasks of those responsible for carrying various parts of the Tabernacle—the Gershonites, Merarites, and the Kohathites. (4:21–49)
- ▸ The text (be warned; this is offensive to modern readers) specifies the way of putting a woman who is suspected of adultery on trial—the *sotah* ritual. She is forced to drink "bitter waters." If her thigh gets distended and distorted, then she is guilty of adultery. If she remains unharmed, then she is innocent. (5:11–29)
- ▸ For those who want to go above and beyond in the holiness department, there is the option of becoming a Nazirite. Nazirites were forbidden to cut their hair; to consume anything alcoholic, or anything that could become intoxicating; and they cannot have any contact with the dead—even their own dead relatives. (6:1–21)
- ▸ God dictates the beautiful priestly blessing to Aaron, the same words that are still used in synagogue today, including at b'nai mitzvah ceremonies and when parents bless children. (6:22–26)
- ▸ At the dedication of the Tabernacle, the prince of each tribe brings gifts as an offering. Each one brings the same gifts. (7:1–87)

The Big Ideas

> **Every Jew has a sacred task to perform.** In the Torah portion, those duties are specific to various families and clans. That is not the way it works anymore. Nowadays, every Jew has to find a particular duty—a mitzvah—that speaks to the heart and that he or she is ready to do.

> **Jealousy is a powerful emotion.** It is absolutely true that marriage is a sacred trust between husband and wife. But something far more disturbing is going on in this passage. The text focuses only on women who are suspected of cheating on their spouses. This seems very unfair; what about husbands who have cheated? (Sad to say, but in the ancient world wives were considered the property of their husbands.) The whole thing starts when a husband becomes suspicious of his wife's actions. The Torah understands the power of jealousy, and in its own way it is trying to figure out how to manage that strong emotion.

> **Holiness should be available to everyone.** The particular characteristics of the Nazirite might seem odd and extreme. But their purpose was to allow the "average" Israelite the same kind of access to holiness as that which was available to the priests. The priesthood was limited to those who were *kohanim,* but anyone could be a *Nazir.* It was "equal opportunity" holiness.

> **People do not bless; God is the ultimate source of blessing.** This is very important. When people utter blessings over food or other things, they must remember that they are not the ones who are making that moment holy. All blessings come from God. And a priestly blessing that goes down from generation to generation ensures that there will be continuity.

> **Every person's contribution is important.** Was it merely a coincidence that each gift the princes brought was identical? Perhaps it was necessary so that they would all feel equal in the eyes of God. But while the gifts were identical, we cannot know what was going on in their hearts and minds—and those feelings and thoughts make each gift different.

Divrei Torah

SO, YOU WANT TO BE A NAZIRITE?

Let's say that you're living in biblical times. Let's say that you wake up one day, and you decide that you want to become a priest, or a Levite, or someone who has the honor and responsibility of carrying the sacred objects of the Tabernacle from place to place as the Israelites moved through the desert. Let's say, later on in biblical history, that you decide you want to become a prophet.

Well, forget about it. You can't. Because all those roles and responsibilities have been designated and assigned by God. There is no "application" process. You either are, or you aren't.

But there was one special thing that you could choose to do—and that was to become a Nazirite.

So, how do you do that? First, you get to be a Nazirite because someone like your mother (see the case of the famous Nazirite named Samson in the book of Judges) makes a vow that you'll be a Nazirite, and it lasts for your whole life. There's not much choice in that. But, apparently, you could also choose on your own to be a Nazirite as well, and for varying amounts of time.

What were the obligations of a Nazirite? No haircuts. No alcohol. No contact with the dead. This last rule is similar to one requirement of the priests, except that priests could have contact with their own dead relatives. Not so for the Nazirite. No contact with the dead—period. In this way, they are being even holier than the priests! (And there may have been other restrictions on the Nazirites that we are not told about in the Torah.)

So, was it "good" to be a Nazirite? It depends on whom you ask. By rejecting pleasure, the Nazirite battled temptation, and that can strengthen one's character. Why couldn't they get haircuts? In ancient times uncut hair, especially since most people then probably didn't wash their hair often, could be a little gross. Which is to say: the Nazirite had to make himself deliberately unattractive.

Why is that? There is a story in the Talmud about a young man with beautiful, curly hair. He chose to become a Nazirite for a very specific reason. "In my native town, I was my father's shepherd. When

I went down to the well, I used to gaze at my reflection in it. That is when I decided to cut off my locks and let my hair go wild." He was in love with the way he looked, and he sensed that this kind of self-absorption and vanity wasn't right.

But not everyone thought that being a Nazirite was such a good idea. Judaism is in favor of legitimate pleasure. Good food, good wine, being attractive—none of those are bad, as long as they are kept in perspective. There are so many prohibitions and restrictions in the Torah—why go and make new ones? Many people probably thought this, and that may be why the Nazirite movement never really caught on in Judaism.

Rabbi Abba Hillel Silver pointed out that the norm of Judaism is to avoid the extreme: "Not a single one of the 613 mitzvot of the Torah enjoins any form of asceticism or mortification upon man. There is but one public fast day ordained in the Torah—Yom Kippur."

One thing is true: the Nazirite devoted his life to things that were higher than pleasure and self-fulfillment. Going above and beyond is not for everyone, but you have to admire people who are trying to live up to high ideals.

OH, NO! NOT ANOTHER ONE!

The kid who becomes bar or bat mitzvah on this Torah portion is in luck. Why? Let's say that your assigned Torah passage consists of the story of the princes' gifts at the Tabernacle's dedication. The prince of every tribe brought precisely the same gift. Yes, it's repetitious—but, on the other hand, there is that much less Hebrew to learn. Learn one set of gifts, and you've learned them all!

But why should this have been the case? Why should all the princes have given the very same gifts? Even more than this: if they all brought the same gifts, why keep mentioning all those princes, and all their gifts?

Centuries ago, Nachmanides, the Spanish Jewish commentator, said: "The Holy One wished to provide equal honor to all the princes by specifying each one's offering on its day, rather than listing the offering of Nahshon ben Amminadab [the first prince to make an offering] and then adding that each of the others had done the same. This would have affected the honor that was due to the others."

Even though the gifts were identical, the Torah wanted to be sure to give credit where it was due. After all, if the princes were going to make the effort to bring their gifts, the Torah should make note of each and every one of them.

Because even though the gifts were all the same, the *givers* were not. The German Orthodox rabbi Shlomo Breuer teaches: "The Torah does not repeat the description of the offerings twelve times in order to teach us that each prince brought exactly the same as every other prince. In fact, they were actually twelve different offerings. This is because what a person gives is not important; how a person gives is important."

In other words, the gifts might have been the same, but each giver had a different attitude toward giving it. One prince might have given enthusiastically; another one might have given with an attitude. For one prince, those gifts might have been very easy to give. For another, not so well off, they might have been a hardship. By listing all these gifts separately, and according to the name of the giver, the Torah is making sure that we understand the uniqueness of every individual, and everyone's gifts.

Connections

➤ Do you think that being a Nazirite was good or bad? Why?

➤ What kinds of pleasures tempt you? Have you ever tried to fight those temptations?

➤ Why do you think that Judaism has always been in favor of people enjoying themselves (within reason and propriety)?

➤ What are the dangers of trying to enjoy yourself too much?

➤ What do you think of the explanation for why all the gifts are listed repeatedly? Do you agree that this was an important thing to do?

➤ Have you ever had the courage to do something first, before anyone else? What was it like?

➤ What are some of the most meaningful gifts that you have given? What are some of the most meaningful gifts that you have received?

➤ What kinds of gifts are nonmaterial? When have you given those types of gifts, and how did you feel about getting them?

THE HAFTARAH

❖ Naso': Judges 13:2–25

Quite often, in the Bible, when children are about to be born, unusual things happen. There is a typical pattern that contains at least one of these elements: the mother-to-be has been struggling with infertility; an angel (a messenger of God) comes and tells her that she will have a child and that the child may grow up to be someone special. This is how it worked with Isaac, son of Abraham and Sarah, and with Samuel, son of Hannah.

This is also how it works with the story of Samson's birth, which is found in this week's haftarah. But there is an additional element: the angel tells Manoah and Mrs. Manoah (his wife is, sadly, unnamed) that their child will be a Nazirite—the link to this week's Torah portion. For that reason, Mrs. Manoah learns that she is not allowed to drink alcoholic beverages during her pregnancy (which is actually a good idea), and that the child will never get his hair cut.

The child of this pregnancy is one of the greatest biblical heroes—the judge Samson, who is blessed with almost superhuman strength. And a few weaknesses, as well . . .

Samson, the First Jewish Superhero

Superheroes were a Jewish invention. The creators of Superman were two Jewish guys from Cleveland, Ohio—Joe Shuster and Jerry Siegel. Where did they get the idea for Superman? One interesting theory is that they were inspired by the story of Samson, the star of this week's haftarah.

It is easy to see why this might be the case. Let's start with Samson's birth, which is a little mysterious, to say the least. An angel of God comes to tell his parents that he will be born, and he will grow up to become a mighty hero, with great strength. The writer Elie Wiesel teaches: "Samson laughed at his enemies, whom he effortlessly vanquished. Nothing frightened him. With one hand he could reduce an entire mountain to dust. His only weakness? Women."

Because Samson is a Nazirite, he is not allowed to cut his hair. And his hair becomes the secret source of his great strength. If it is cut, he will become weakened, sort of like the threat of kryptonite to Superman.

Samson is unique; he is a different kind of Jewish hero. Traditionally, Jews identify heroism not in what you are able to do with your physical strength, but with moral and ethical heroism. The Mishnah teaches: "Who is a hero? He who resists his temptations." Even though Jews believe that the body is precious and that we should take care of ourselves to stay healthy, physical strength has never been a big Jewish value. In traditional Jewish life, the only time that you really need physical strength is to lift the Torah—which, when you open it up to reveal the sacred writing on the parchment, is very heavy!

For centuries, Jews thought that mental, moral, and spiritual strength were enough. But the birth of the State of Israel demonstrated that Jews had to be physically strong as well, strong like Samson. The Zionist leader Vladimir (Ze'ev) Jabotinsky wrote a novel about Samson, and in his book Samson derives his physical strength from his hair, but he also admires and learns from the military strength of his enemy, the Philistines. These are Samson's last words, as imagined by Jabotinsky: "Get hold of iron. Give whatever you have for it. The second [thing you need] is a king. One person, at a signal from whom thousands will raise their arms all at once."

Samson's story does not end well. Ultimately, he is betrayed by Delilah, who turns him over to the Philistines. She seduces him and learns his secret; then she cuts his hair. The Philistines imprison and blind him. When his hair starts to grow back, Samson pulls down the pillars of a Philistine temple, killing many Philistines, along with himself.

Samson is physically powerful, but he becomes emotionally and morally blind (by allowing himself to be seduced) before he becomes physically blind. What is the story trying to teach us? Without vision and wisdom, physical strength and power are meaningless—sometimes even lethal. Samson is a hero, but an incomplete hero. He is the first to save Israel from the Philistines, but he's not the last. Samson's end is tragic, and his work is unfinished. Every generation has to do its part. And every person needs to be strong internally, if not externally.

❖ Notes

❖ Notes

9 780827 614208